D0712943

SNOWY OWLS

by Jennifer Zeiger

Content Consultant
Dr. Stephen S. Ditchkoff
Professor of Wildlife Sciences
Auburn University
Auburn, Alabama

Photographs © 2014: age fotostock: 40, 41 (Mark Duffy), 12, 13
(W Layer); Alamy Images: 5 bottom inset, 38, 39 (Bruce Corbett),
32 (Kanwarjit Singh Boparai/DVM); Bob Italiano: 44 map, 45
map; Dreamstime: 5 top inset, 24 (Colette6), 35 (Czbrat), 1, 10,
11, 46 (Jimwalling), 2 owl, 3 owl, 22, 23 (Mdockery), 36, 37
(Montagumontgomery), 2 background, 3 background,
44 background, 45 background; Nature Picture
Library: 26, 27 (Markus Varesvuo), 6, 7
(Staffan Widstrand); Science Source/Jim Zipp:
cover, 4, 5 background, 14, 15; Superstock,
Inc.: 20, 21 (Bruce J Lichtenberge), 30, 31
(FLPA), 28, 29 (Minden Pictures), 8 (Steven
Kazlowski), 16, 17, 18, 19 (Wayne Lynch).

Library of Congress Cataloging-in-Publication Data
Zeiger, Jennifer.
 Snowy owls / by Jennifer Zeiger.
 pages cm. — (Nature's children)
 Audience: Grade 4 to 6.
 Includes bibliographical references and index.
 ISBN 978-0-531-21228-8 (lib. bdg.) — ISBN 978-0-531-25438-7
(paperback)
 1. Snowy owl—Juvenile literature. I. Title.
 QL696.S83Z45 2014
 598.9'7—dc23
 2013021991

All rights reserved. Published in 2014 by Children's Press, an imprint
of Scholastic Inc.

5499 3083
11/14

Printed in China 62
SCHOLASTIC, CHILDREN'S PRESS, and associated logos are
trademarks and/or registered trademarks of Scholastic Inc.

1 2 3 4 5 6 7 8 9 10 R 23 22 21 20 19 18 17 16 15 14

Snowy Owls

Class	Aves
Order	Strigiformes
Family	Strigidae
Genus	Bubo
Species	Bubo scandiacus
World distribution	Mainly found north of the Arctic Circle in Canada, Alaska, Greenland, Iceland, Scandinavian countries, and Russia; in winter, also found farther south
Habitat	Most common in open tundra areas; also live in meadows, marshes, farmland, and coastal areas
Distinctive physical characteristics	Females can weigh up to 6.5 pounds (3 kilograms); males weigh about 5.5 pounds (2.5 kg) or less; wingspan can measure up to 5 feet (1.5 meters); white feathers with black or brown spots or bar-shaped markings; large yellow eyes outlined by black eyelids; small ear tufts
Habits	Fly silently to sneak up on prey; dive-bomb to defend territories from other owls; raise feathers and stretch wings to appear larger and intimidate enemies; migrate seasonally to follow prey; generally solitary, except during mating season; active during the day, unlike most other owl species
Diet	Mainly eat lemmings; also eat voles, hares, other small mammals, and birds; occasionally eat amphibians, fish, insects, and crustaceans

Snowy Owls

CHAPTER 1

Arctic Owls

Far north into the Arctic, a female snowy owl sits on a low rise in the landscape. The spotted white bird is barely visible among the rocks and snow. Underneath the owl's body, four white eggs are sheltered from the wind and cold. A male owl stands guard nearby. Its large yellow eyes scan the area for prey and possible danger.

The male owl turns its head to look as it hears a sound from the east. An Arctic fox crouches there, watching the female sitting on the nest. The hungry fox must be looking for a meal. Thinking fast, the male snowy owl takes off and flies high into the air. Before the fox can move, the owl changes course and dives straight down. It attacks the predator in a flurry of feathers, beak, and talons. Scared and hurt, the fox runs off. The snowy owls and their young are safe once again.

A snowy owl is almost completely invisible against the icy backdrop of its Arctic home.

Big Birds

The snowy owl is the heaviest owl in North America. It is also one of the heaviest in the world. Females can weigh up to 6.5 pounds (3 kilograms). Males are slightly smaller, weighing about 5.5 pounds (2.5 kg) or less. The owl's long wings can stretch up to 5 feet (1.5 meters) from wingtip to wingtip.

The snowy owl's bulky body is thickly covered in light-colored feathers. These owls are named for their coloring. Their feathers are mostly white, with spots or bar-shaped markings that are black or brown. Males have fewer markings than females do. The markings become lighter as an owl grows older. A male's markings may eventually disappear altogether. A snowy owl's large yellow eyes are outlined by black eyelids. Its head is round with ear tufts so small that they are often hidden within the owl's feathers.

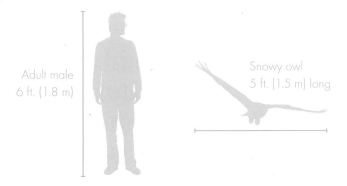

Adult male
6 ft. (1.8 m)

Snowy owl
5 ft. (1.5 m) long

A snowy owl's dark spots help it blend in with rocks and dirt that stick out from the snow.

CHAPTER 2

Fierce Flyers

Feathers are important to a snowy owl's survival for many reasons. They are shaped to allow the owl to fly. Most birds make a sound as they flap their wings, but owl feathers are different. Their edges are serrated. This muffles the sound of their wing beats, making an owl's flight silent. This helps the owl sneak up on its prey.

The snowy owl's feathers also keep the bird warm in the cold Arctic weather. They extend from the owl's head to its toes and form a dense, insulating covering that helps keep heat from escaping the owl's body. The feathers' spotted white coloring is useful. It acts as camouflage. The feathers blend in with the snow and the occasional rocks of the owl's home. This allows the owl to hide from its prey and any possible predators.

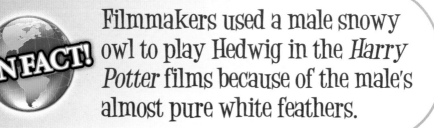

FUN FACT! Filmmakers used a male snowy owl to play Hedwig in the *Harry Potter* films because of the male's almost pure white feathers.

Silent flight prevents potential prey from noticing an incoming snowy owl.

Eyes and Ears

Incredibly sharp eyesight and hearing help snowy owls find prey. A snowy owl's eyesight and hearing are so good that it can track prey underneath snow or thick vegetation. The owl's head is wide for a bird. This provides plenty of room for its large eyes. The eyes cannot move very much in their sockets. This means owls cannot move their eyes to look around as humans can. Instead, owls look around by moving their heads. Snowy owls can turn their heads almost completely around.

A snowy owl's ears are large but hidden beneath feathers. The feathers covering the owl's ear openings are lacy. This allows sound to easily pass through to the ear. The feathers around the edges of the owl's ears are shaped to increase a sound's volume, much like a bell. The ears are also set unevenly on the owl's head. This enables the owl to pinpoint a sound's location by comparing the differences in each ear.

Snowy owls can twist their heads to incredible angles, allowing them to see their entire surroundings.

Beak and Talons

A snowy owl's beak and talons are made to grip and tear. Its dark beak is short and sharp. It is almost completely hidden by the surrounding feathers. When the owl hunts, it uses its beak to grip its prey before swallowing it whole. If the prey is too large to swallow whole, an owl can use its beak to tear off bites.

Snowy owls have four toes on each of their two feet. Each toe ends in a long, curved talon that is as sharp as a needle. A snowy owl's talons are strong for a bird of its size. When the owl catches prey, the talons help keep it from escaping. In addition, the owl's outer toes can point either outward or completely backward. This wide spread gives the owl an excellent grip when picking up prey.

FUN FACT! Snowy owls might hunt at any time during the 24 hours of daylight during the Arctic summer.

A snowy owl uses its sharp talons to snatch unsuspecting prey from the ground.

A Strong Defense

Snowy owls are deadly hunters. However, they must defend themselves from attackers. Snowy owls face several predators in the Arctic. Among them are foxes, wolves, dogs, coyotes, and jaegers, which are a type of bird. The owls must also defend their territories from other snowy owls.

One way snowy owls defend themselves and their territories is by dive-bombing. They fly up and then swiftly down at an animal to attack it. Snowy owls can be bold when they feel threatened. They have even been known to dive-bomb large animals such as humans and wolves.

Snowy owls often use a threatening pose to frighten other owls out of a territory. The threatening owl lowers its head and sticks it out to the front. It also raises its neck feathers and stretches out its wings. This posture makes the owl appear larger than it is. The outsider is often scared away.

An owl's puffed-up, threatening posture is all it takes to frighten off most enemies.

CHAPTER 3

Life Around the Arctic Circle

Snowy owls are found all around the world in the north. Their summer home is above the Arctic Circle. Here, the sun never sets for several weeks in the summer and never rises for several weeks in the winter. Unlike most owls, snowy owls are **diurnal**, so the endless summer days do not bother them The owls sometimes **migrate** south during the winter. There, the weather is somewhat warmer and food is easier to find. However, these areas are still very cold.

Snowy owls prefer wide-open areas. In the Arctic, the birds are found in the treeless tundra. Their homes are often near the shores of oceans or lakes. Farther south, they stay in meadows, marshes, farmland, or occasionally **urban** areas. They especially like land that is rolling with low hills. They also like areas that have fences, buildings, or other high places to perch. There, a snowy owl can sit with a good view of the surrounding land, watching for prey and predators.

Even a snowy owl's southern winter habitat is often covered in snow.

Lemmings and Other Tasty Treats

Snowy owls are **carnivores**. Their favorite meal is a lemming. A snowy owl can eat as many as 1,600 of these small **rodents** in a single year. Owls also catch other small mammals such as rabbits, hares, and weasels. They eat amphibians such as frogs and toads. They also hunt insects and birds. When prey is small enough, the owl swallows it whole. Later it **regurgitates** bones, fur, and anything else that cannot be digested in a compact **pellet**.

A snowy owl might sit for hours watching and listening for prey. The owl makes sure it knows what kind of animal its potential prey is before going after it. Then the owl may fly low over the ground and pounce on its prey. When catching a frog or toad, the owl might hover above before snatching it from the water. A snowy owl can catch a bird right out of the air in midflight.

FUN FACT! A snowy owl sometimes stores extra food in a stash near its perch.

A snowy owl hones in on a lemming. There are 20 different lemming species around the world.

Occasional Migration

Food determines where a snowy owl lives during the year. This means the owls usually go where they can find the most lemmings. In summer, lemmings are plentiful in the tundra. The owls have no problem finding enough to eat in their territories in Canada, Alaska, Greenland, northern Russia, Sweden, Norway, Iceland, and Denmark. Sometimes lemming and other local prey populations are still high in the Arctic during winter. In these years, snowy owls remain in the Arctic all year.

Often, however, prey populations decrease in the winter. When this happens, snowy owls migrate south, to the northern United States, central Europe and Russia, and sometimes central Asia. About every four years, the number of lemmings drops considerably. This forces snowy owls to move even farther south. In particularly extreme years, snowy owls have been spotted as far south as Texas, Florida, and Japan.

Snowy owls spread their wings wide to glide along the ground.

Living and Communicating

Snowy owls tend to spend their winters alone. Males and females defend their territories from other owls. The size of these territories depends on how much food is available. Snowy owl territories tend to be small when there is a lot of food to go around. When food is scarce, territories need to be larger so owls can find enough to eat. Male and female owls come together in spring and summer to form breeding pairs and establish summer territories. These pairs tend to be monogamous. This means the male and female do not mate with other owls during a breeding season.

Snowy owls are mostly silent when they are alone during the winter. Often, the only sounds they make are deep hoots to scare other owls away from their territory. During the summer, however, owls use a range of sounds. They might hiss, mew, or cackle. Sometimes they make a "kre-kre" or "rick-rick" call. Scientists believe these sounds are most often used when a predator approaches the owl's nest.

Snowy owls form close bonds with their mates.

Finding a Place to Breed

Snowy owls head north to breeding grounds when the weather warms in the spring. They only breed when there is enough food to feed their young. Some owls may breed only every three to five years.

The male owl performs a dramatic mating display when a male and a female owl come together as a breeding pair. It first takes off in an exaggerated flight upward. It often carries a lemming in its beak or its talons as it does this. Then it flies back down, either flapping its wings or holding them up in a V-shape. On the ground, the male turns its back to the female and bows low as it fans out its tail.

Snowy owls usually begin to arrive at their breeding grounds in April. Between May and September, the owls mate, lay eggs, and raise their young. When a breeding pair arrives on the tundra, the male chooses a territory. Then the female chooses where in the territory to build a nest.

A male snowy owl brings food to its mate back at the nest.

Building a Home

It takes a few days for a female snowy owl to build a nest. For this reason, snowy owls might return to the same nest each summer for many years. The female first finds a low viewpoint, such as a boulder or hill, in the breeding territory. A good nesting place needs to have enough wind to keep the area dry and clear of snow. Once she finds the perfect place, she scratches a shallow hole in the ground. She then lies down in the hole to shape it.

The number of eggs she lays depends on food availability. Usually, a **brood** can include between 3 and 6 eggs. However, an owl can lay as many as 11 eggs when there are lots of lemmings in the area. The mother only lays one egg at a time. The eggs are often laid two or three days apart. The nest is not lined with grass or other insulation. Instead, the female **incubates** the eggs by sitting on them.

FUN FACT! Snow geese sometimes nest near snowy owls to benefit from their defense from predators.

Newly hatched snowy owls are covered in fuzzy feathers that make them look very different from their parents.

Growing Up

Incubation lasts about 31 days. Because the eggs are laid one at a time, they hatch separately. Owl chicks are wet and blind when they hatch. Their soft, downy feathers dry after a couple of hours. The chicks are covered in dark spots and bars. These shapes fade as the chicks grow older. After five days, they open their eyes.

The chicks begin to explore outside the nest after two to four weeks. However, they cannot fly until they are around eight weeks old. Even after they start flying, chicks stay near the nest until they can hunt for themselves. Both parents help protect the nest. The father also hunts. He brings food back to the mother. She tears it into smaller pieces for the chicks to eat. Chicks and parents each go their own way at the end of summer. When they are about two years old, the young owls are ready to breed. In the wild, a snowy owl can live up to 9 years. Captive owls may live more than 20 years.

FUN FACT! If a nesting attempt fails, a breeding pair may try to start another one.

Young snowy owls quickly begin growing larger and stronger.

CHAPTER 4

Birds of Prey

Scientists study **fossils** of owls and other birds to learn about ancient **species**. They believe that owls first developed more than 65 million years ago. This was after dinosaurs disappeared. Over the next 10 million to 30 million years, owls developed into many different species.

Owls have changed somewhat since then. Some ancient owls were much larger than the owls seen today. One ancient barn owl found in Puerto Rico was about twice the size of modern barn owls. This owl died out about 11,700 years ago. Many ancient owls, including snowy owls, may have had much larger ranges. Scientists have found fossils of owls related to modern snowy owls as far south as the tropics. Some experts believe snowy owls might have originally developed in that region.

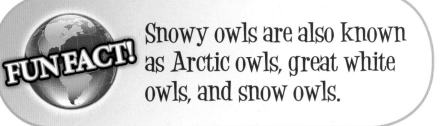

FUN FACT! Snowy owls are also known as Arctic owls, great white owls, and snow owls.

Fossils have helped scientists learn a great deal about ancient owl species.

Close Relatives

There is only one species of snowy owl. It is part of the **genus** *Bubo*. This genus also includes horned owls, such as eagle owls and the great horned owl. Despite their close relation, most horned owls are very different from snowy owls. Like most other owls, horned owls tend to be **nocturnal**. They also tend to have large, clearly visible ear tufts. Some scientists argue that these tufts are for camouflage. Without the ear tufts, the owl's head would be a cleanly curved surface. This shape could be noticed easily among sticks, leaves, and other vegetation. Ear tufts break this shape, helping the curved head blend in with its surroundings.

One thing snowy owls and horned owls have in common is size. Horned owls tend to be quite large. The great horned owl has a wingspan of up to 4.8 feet (1.5 m). Its body is even larger than that of the snowy owl. However, the snowy owl is heavier because of its thick feathers.

The great horned owl is one of the world's largest owl species.

Nighttime Hunters

Owls are a hugely varied group of birds. They are found nearly everywhere except for Antarctica. All owls are part of the order Strigiformes. They might be as large as great horned owls or as small as elf owls, which are about the size of sparrows. The most obvious feature all owl species share is their eyes, which always point forward. Most birds' eyes are positioned on the sides of their heads.

Despite most species being nocturnal, all owls are visual hunters. Their eyes are quite large for birds, which helps them see in the dark. As birds of prey, their talons are long and sharp. Their beaks curve sharply down to grasp prey.

Most owls, including snowy owls, are part of the Strigidae family. Barn owls are part of a separate group, along with grass owls and bay owls. These species look slightly different from other owls. The difference is most noticeably in the owls' faces. Though all owls have relatively flat face disks, barn owls and their relatives have heart-shaped faces.

A barn owl's face shape helps set it apart from most other kinds of owls.

CHAPTER 5

Remote Creatures

Snowy owls are nomads. They settle wherever prey is available and often move unpredictably. This makes it difficult for scientists to study them. In addition, the owls spend most of their time in remote places. This makes them difficult to reach in the wild. As a result, scientists do not have as much information about snowy owls as they do about other kinds of owls. Experts are not sure how many snowy owls there currently are, but they estimate there are more than 300,000. There may be as many as 10,000 breeding pairs in Russia alone.

Thanks to their large numbers and wide range, snowy owls are not endangered. However, studies have indicated that their numbers are slowly decreasing. The decrease is too slow for scientists to be worried yet. But if the decline continues, the state of snowy owls may change.

Snowy owls are not in danger of dying out in the near future.

Living Together

Snowy owls' remoteness means that they have little contact with humans. This does not mean that humans do not affect them. Snowy owls sometimes run into power lines or are hit and killed by cars or even airplanes. Snowy owls can also become tangled up in fishing lines. The owls occasionally raid traplines to take the bait left by hunters to catch other animals. In response, hunters might shoot the owls to protect their traps. In some locations, native groups hunt snowy owls for food or feathers. Few owls are killed this way, however, so the hunting has little effect on owl populations.

Snowy owls are protected by a number of laws around the world. Many people are also studying ways to keep snowy owls and other birds safe from airplanes and power lines. These laws and changes indicate a promising future for snowy owls. Perhaps one day you may be able to see a snowy owl yourself!

Snowy owls sometimes perch on power lines near human settlements.

Words to Know

breeding (BREE-ding) — mating and giving birth to young

brood (BROOD) — a group of young birds that all hatched at the same time

camouflage (KAM-uh-flahzh) — a disguise or a natural coloring that allows animals, people, or objects to hide by making them look like their surroundings

captive (KAP-tiv) — confined to a place and not able to escape

carnivores (KAHR-nuh-vorz) — animals that eat meat

diurnal (dye-URN-uhl) — describing an animal that is typically active during the day and asleep at night

endangered (en-DAYN-jurd) — at risk of becoming extinct, usually because of human activity

fossils (FAH-suhlz) — bones, shells, or other traces of animals or plants from long ago, preserved as rock

genus (JEE-nuhs) — a group of related plants or animals that is larger than a species but smaller than a family

incubates (ING-kyuh-bates) — keeps eggs warm before they hatch

insulating (IN-suh-lay-ting) — stopping heat from escaping

mate (MATE) — to join together to produce babies

migrate (MYE-grate) — to move to another area or climate at a particular time of year

monogamous (muh-NAH-guh-muhs) — describing an animal that stays with the same mate

nocturnal (nahk-TUR-nuhl) — active mainly at night

nomads (NOH-madz) — animals that wander from place to place

order (OR-dur) — a group of related plants or animals that is bigger than a family but smaller than a class

pellet (PEL-it) — a small, hard ball of material that could not be digested by a bird of prey

predator (PRED-uh-tur) — an animal that lives by hunting other animals for food

prey (PRAY) — an animal that's hunted by another animal for food

regurgitates (ri-GUR-juh-tates) — brings food that has been swallowed back up to the mouth

rodents (ROH-duhnts) — mammals with large, sharp front teeth that are used for gnawing

serrated (SER-ay-tid) — having a jagged edge

species (SPEE-sheez) — one of the groups into which animals and plants of the same genus are divided; members of the same species can mate and have offspring

talons (TAL-uhns) — sharp claws of a bird

territories (TER-uh-tor-eez) — areas of land claimed by animals

urban (UR-buhn) — having to do with a city

Habitat Map

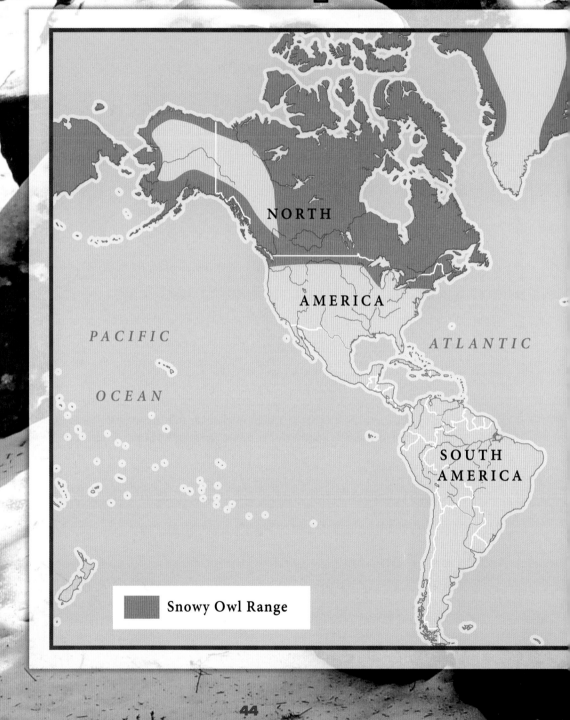

NORTH

AMERICA

SOUTH
AMERICA

PACIFIC

OCEAN

ATLANTIC

Snowy Owl Range

ARCTIC OCEAN

EUROPE

ASIA

AFRICA

PACIFIC OCEAN

INDIAN OCEAN

OCEAN

AUSTRALIA

Find Out More

Books

Gregory, Josh. *Owls*. New York: Children's Press, 2013.

Owen, Ruth. *Snowy Owls*. New York: Windmill Books, 2013.

Read, Tracy C. *Exploring the World of Owls*. Richmond Hill, ON: Firefly Books, 2011.

Visit this Scholastic Web site for more information on snowy owls:
www.factsfornow.scholastic.com
Enter the keywords **Snowy Owls**

Index

Page numbers in *italics* indicate a photograph or map.

About the Author

Jennifer Zeiger lives in Chicago, Illinois, where she writes and edits books for children. She has always been interested in birds, and the snowy owl is one of her favorites!